Kitchen Lab

Michael Elsohn Ross

with illustrations by Tim Seeley

Carolrhoda Books, Inc./Minneapolis

To the Tierneys
—M. E. R.

To Gina Crone, for all she is and will be
—T. S.

Each experiment described in this book is intended solely for the purpose of illustrating the scientific principles and concepts identified with that experiment. The experiments should not be performed in any manner or for any purpose other than as described herein. The publisher and the author specifically disclaim any liability for any injury, damage, or loss sustained, directly or indirectly, as a result of the application or use of any experiment for any other purpose, or the performance of any experiment other than in strict accordance with the instructions contained herein.

Carolrhoda Books, Inc.
A division of Lerner Publishing Group
241 First Avenue North, Minneapolis, MN 55401 U.S.A.

Website address: www.lernerbooks.com

Library of Congress Cataloging-in-Publication Data

Ross, Michael Elsohn, 1952-
Kitchen lab / by Michael Elsohn Ross ; with illustrations by Tim Seeley.
p. cm. — (You are the scientist)
Includes index.
Summary: Discusses the scientific method of investigation and describes various experiments that can be done using ingredients or tools found in a kitchen.
ISBN: 0–87614–625–6 (lib. bdg. : alk. paper)
1. Science—Experiments—Juvenile literature. [1. Science—Experiments. 2. Experiments.] I. Seeley, Tim, ill. II. Title.
Q164 .R675 2003
507'.8–dc21 2001006132

Manufactured in the United States of America
1 2 3 4 5 6 – JR – 08 07 06 05 04 03

TABLE OF CONTENTS

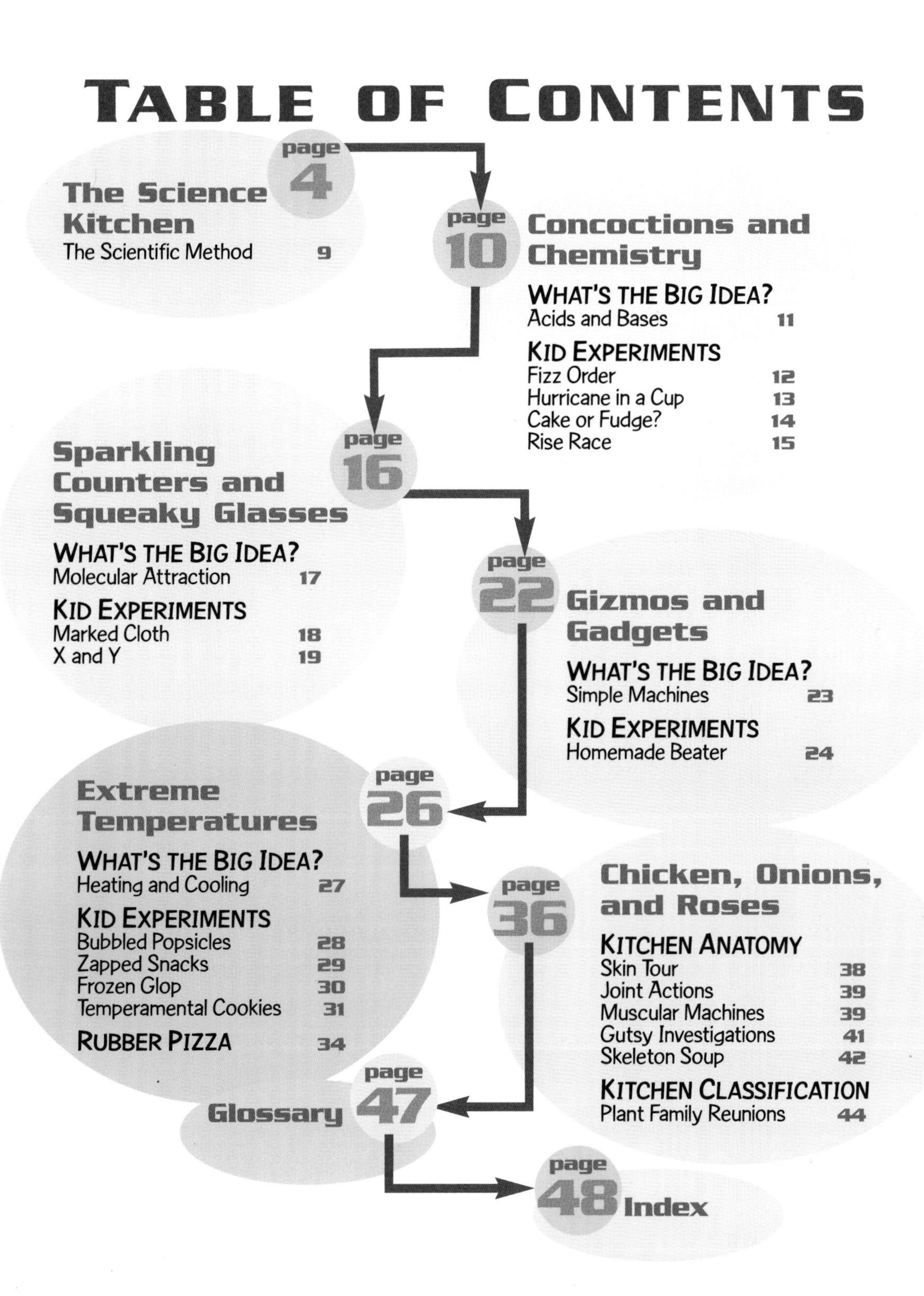

page 4 The Science Kitchen
The Scientific Method 9

page 10 Concoctions and Chemistry
WHAT'S THE BIG IDEA?
Acids and Bases 11
KID EXPERIMENTS
Fizz Order 12
Hurricane in a Cup 13
Cake or Fudge? 14
Rise Race 15

page 16 Sparkling Counters and Squeaky Glasses
WHAT'S THE BIG IDEA?
Molecular Attraction 17
KID EXPERIMENTS
Marked Cloth 18
X and Y 19

page 22 Gizmos and Gadgets
WHAT'S THE BIG IDEA?
Simple Machines 23
KID EXPERIMENTS
Homemade Beater 24

page 26 Extreme Temperatures
WHAT'S THE BIG IDEA?
Heating and Cooling 27
KID EXPERIMENTS
Bubbled Popsicles 28
Zapped Snacks 29
Frozen Glop 30
Temperamental Cookies 31
RUBBER PIZZA 34

page 36 Chicken, Onions, and Roses
KITCHEN ANATOMY
Skin Tour 38
Joint Actions 39
Muscular Machines 39
Gutsy Investigations 41
Skeleton Soup 42
KITCHEN CLASSIFICATION
Plant Family Reunions 44

page 47 Glossary

page 48 Index

The Science Kitchen

Like most folks, you probably think of the kitchen as a place to find food and prepare meals. Kitchens can also be secret scientific labs where curious cooks carry on experiments. Have you ever created weird potions? Do you experiment with new recipes? Have you ever found yourself conducting a scientific test without really intending to? Perhaps you were finding out how to make bigger bubbles while you washed dishes. Maybe you were testing how long it would take for your cereal to get soggy. Experiments can just happen or they can grow from questions, challenges, or comparisons, or by trying to solve problems.

New foods, cooking methods, and even kitchen gadgets are often the result of curious kitchen scientists at play. A kitchen has many of the same tools and equipment as a science lab. There are counters, a sink, burners on your stove, mixing bowls, and jars of strange substances. Explorations in the kitchen can produce new concoctions or tools, but they can also reveal big ideas, like how molecules behave. When you start to explore, you may be opening the cupboard to scientific mysteries.

YOUR LABORATORY

Any kitchen can become an official research lab. Of course, sometimes you may find yourself exploring in the wrong kitchen at the wrong time. Here are some basic tips to make your investigations as much appreciated as a well-baked cake:

- Ask permission before you use someone's kitchen ingredients or equipment. (For example, get the OK before you mix your dad's favorite mustard with soda pop.)
- Consider how the experiment might affect kitchen equipment. Think carefully before you do something that might damage your kitchen or the tools in it.
- **Do not** do any tests with matches, the stove, the oven, sharp knives, or anything else dangerous unless you are supervised by a **responsible adult.**

- Alert other members of your household to experiments in progress by making a sign that states there is an important kitchen experiment in action!
- To tune your folks in to the importance of kitchen explorations, show them the following article from the fictional newspaper column "Popular Scientists."

From Ice Cubes to the Antarctic

by Fridga Daire

Auckland, New Zealand: Explorer Henrique Lopez announced the opening of his new international research center near the South Pole today. Since he began his cool studies of glacial ice ten years ago, he has made great discoveries about the formation of the earth and the changing climates of the last few million years. When asked how he got so interested in ice, Lopez remarked, "It all began when I was just a kid fooling around in the kitchen during hot summer days. My grandmother let me use her freezer for experiments. It kept me cool, but more importantly, it allowed me to follow my questions."

Lopez has led investigations in all of the world's coldest places, including Mount Everest and Baffin Island, but he feels he has barely explored past the tip of the iceberg when it comes to understanding the secrets of the world's vast ice fields.

"It's like defrosting my grandmother's freezer. You never knew what you would find."

QUESTIONS EVERYWHERE Some folks are constantly asking questions: What happens if you make oatmeal with apple juice? How does a can opener work? What kinds of liquids make baking soda fizz? People who follow questions may find themselves on the path of scientific exploration. Like other curious explorers who have gone before, you may not know where you are headed, but you have a reason to get started. Experiments grow from questions. Listen to your questions and let them push you into adventure!

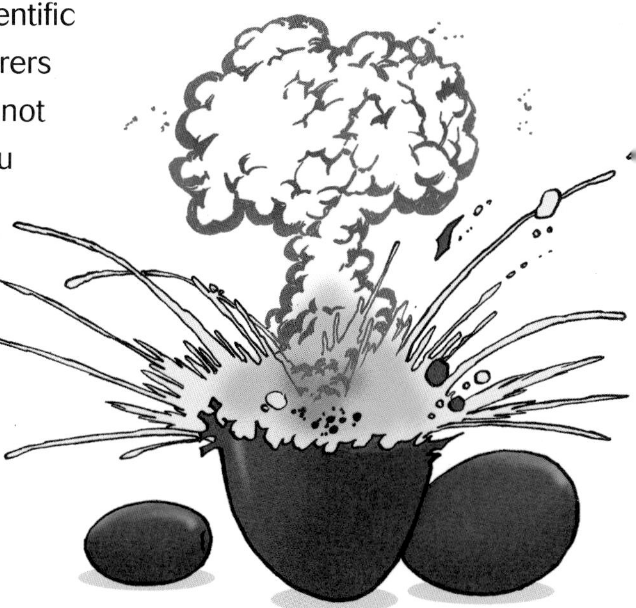

Here are some questions from kids at El Portal Elementary School:

- Will bubbles freeze?
- Will one brand of detergent really clean better than another?
- Can we invent our own cake recipe?
- How does yeast grow in different mixes?
- How will colors blend in different mixes of stuff?
- Will a grape explode when heated in a microwave?
- Which materials dissolve in water?
- Which baking soda mix will rise highest?
- Can we invent our own electric mixer?
- Will changing the oven temperature make homemade cookies bake differently?
- Can you freeze sugar?

What If . . .

What if I mixed soda and oil? Would the soda still bubble? What if I left milk out overnight? Would it turn sour? Tune in to these "what if" wonderings. Design tests to find out what happens.

- Use fair tests. For example, if you are testing to see which of two cleansers works better, think about how you would use each cleanser. It definitely wouldn't be fair if you scrubbed harder with one than with the other, would it?
- Perform your test several times to see if the same thing happens every time.
- Record what happens by taking notes, pictures, or video footage.
- Share your results with friends and family, and challenge them to repeat your test to see if they get the same results. (Your results might help them make wiser choices the next time they go shopping!)

To the Drawing Board Some tests lead to new designs. Could you come up with a new recipe for chocolate chip cookies? Did you ever wonder how cooks come up with new recipes or inventions for new kitchen tools? Like a gourmet chef, you can make changes in the way you cook to see if you can cook better.

- Try experiments with different ways to store food or to clean up kitchen messes.
- Choose one part of a recipe to change at a time. That way you will know what effect the change has on how the food comes out. If you change too many things at once, you will be clueless about which change really made the difference.
- Repeat your test several times to see if the change you made in the recipe produces the same results each time.

THE SCIENTIFIC METHOD

The scientific method is like a recipe for discovery. As you investigate kitchen mysteries, try the following recipe and see what you cook up!

1. Start with a question or guess. (For example: I think ice cubes with a pebble in them will take longer to melt than regular ice cubes.) Write it down. Keep a lab notebook.
2. Test. (For example: Make a tray of ice cubes with a pebble in each cube compartment and another tray with just water. Freeze both and then place one pebble cube and one regular cube in separate bowls. Watch them to see which melts first.) Record your results.
3. Repeat, repeat, repeat! Do your test several times under the same conditions to see if the same things happen. Write down what happens each time so you can compare.
4. Draw a conclusion. Why do you think you got the results you did? Jot down your ideas.
5. Modify and retest. If you feel like it, you can change the test slightly and do it over. (For example: Put the ice cubes in water and watch to see which cube melts first.) Remember to change only one part of your test at a time so the results are clear.

As you mess around in the kitchen, any experiment that you come up with will help you learn something new. That's the great thing about experiments. Whether they deliver the answer you were looking for or not, you always end up with something, even if it's another mystery.

Concoctions and Chemistry

Like a real chemistry lab, kitchen cupboards contain a wild array of substances. There are oils to grease our pans and detergents to wash the oils away. There are tart, stinging acids, such as vinegar and lemon juice. There are bases, such as baking powder and antacids. Bases neutralize acids by uniting with them to produce salts. We use these chemicals every day, but we don't always experiment with them. With the head cook's OK, go explore some kitchen chemistry. Mix up some potions and see where they lead. Just be careful not to leave around any bubbling messes or oozing goo that could get you into trouble.

ACIDS AND BASES For ages, people classified substances as acids or bases by feel and taste alone. Acids, such as vinegar, lime juice, and aspirin, are noticeably sour. The word "acid" comes from "acetum," the Latin word for vinegar. Acids turn blue litmus paper red. Many acids are strong enough to dissolve metals or rocks.

Bases are noted for their soapy or slippery texture and bitter taste. Many bases, such as bleach, drain cleaner, and lye, are poisonous, so it's not a good idea to taste them. Bases turn red litmus paper blue.

The pH scale is used to describe the strength of acids and bases. A substance with a pH of 7, such as pure water, is neutral. Acids have a pH less than 7. Bases have a pH greater than 7.

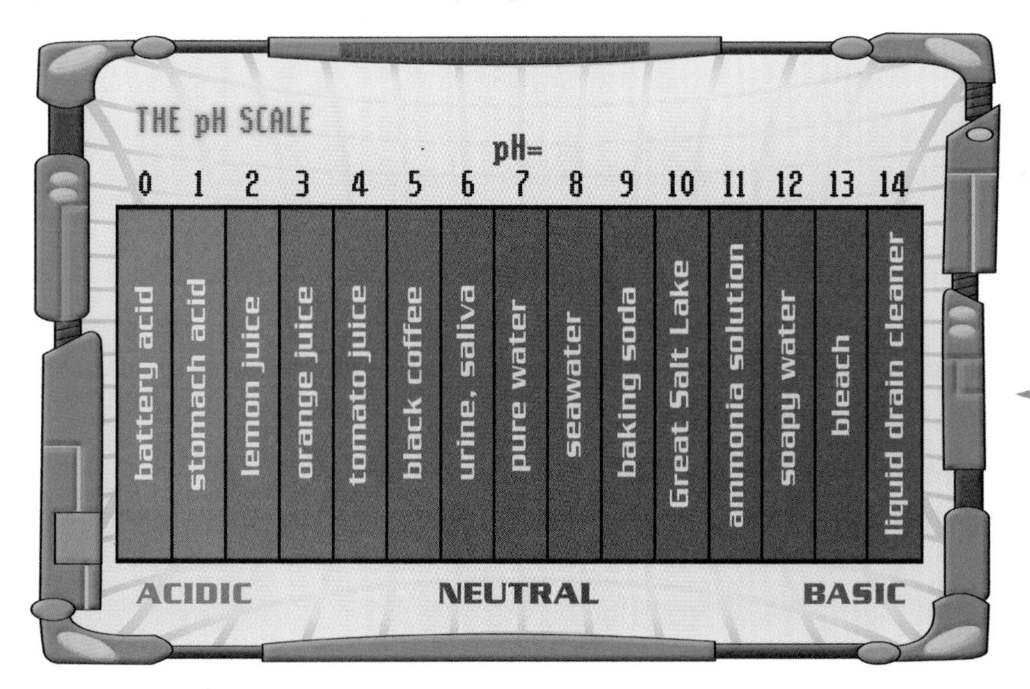

KID Experiments

FIZZ ORDER Since kindergarten, Nick and Rico have played with baking soda and vinegar. Long ago, they discovered that combining vinegar and baking soda creates bubbles. Now that they were fifth graders, they wondered if the order in which they mixed these substances would make a difference in the fizzing.

To start with, they placed a tablespoon of baking soda (sodium bicarbonate) in a bowl and then poured a tablespoonful of vinegar over the soda. As soon as the vinegar hit the soda, the vinegar started to bubble and fizz and foam out over the top. Within a short time, the fizz fizzled out and the foam died down.

Next, they poured a tablespoonful of vinegar in a bowl and then added the baking soda to it. Big bubbles formed, but the foam didn't go as high. The baking soda dissolved slowly, and the fizzing lasted longer. Even after a few minutes, there was still a mound of baking soda in the bottom of the bowl.

The boys figured there was less of a reaction when the baking soda was dumped in the vinegar because the baking soda could not dissolve as quickly. It only fizzed along the outer edges where the vinegar could touch it. When the vinegar was poured on the baking soda, it soaked up all the baking soda and reacted all at once.

What do you think?

HURRICANE IN A CUP How do colors mix in different potions? Rhyen mixed several potions. He used the same temperature water for each test. He dropped yellow food coloring into each potion, adding it in the center of the cup. Then he added red, too. This is what Rhyen observed:

POTION	RESULTS
1. baking soda, salt, water	The dark yellow made a swirl like a hurricane. It faded to a lighter yellow at the edges of the cup. The red made a swirl in the center of the yellow swirl and turned orange at the edges.
2. baking soda, water	The same thing happened as with potion #1.
3. salt, water	The water stayed clear around the edges of the cup, and the red sank to the bottom of the cup. There was no swirl.
4. plain water	There were no swirls, and the colors stayed in the center.

Rhyen tried this test several times, and the same thing happened each time. He assumed there are special ingredients in baking soda that help it hold the colors, but had no clues what those ingredients are. Do you have any ideas?

CAKE OR FUDGE? Some people like to change recipes, and others invent new ones. David and Josh set to work one evening in the kitchen to create a new cake recipe. They knew that baking soda makes cakes rise. Their improved formula included more baking soda and eggs than other recipes, but less butter. This is what they used:

CAKE OR FUDGE? RECIPE

2 tbsp. butter
3 eggs
½ cup water
1 cup sugar
½ cup cocoa powder
1 ½ cup flour
1 tbsp. baking soda

They mixed the butter, eggs, and water together, then added the rest of the ingredients. They put the batter in a pan and baked it. It bubbled while it was baking and they could see it rising until it got huge. After the boys took the cake out of the oven and let it cool, they decorated it with store-bought icing and sprinkles. The kids in their class liked it. David said it tasted more like fudge than like a spongy cake. Josh thought that using more eggs made the cake thicker and fudgier. Perhaps you can experiment with the number of eggs and amount of baking soda in a cake or cookie recipe and see what happens to the final product. What makes a fudgier treat—more eggs or more baking soda, or both?

RISE RACE Besides baking soda and baking powder (a combination of baking soda and cream of tartar), yeast is used to make baked goods rise. Yeast isn't a base, though. Yeast is actually a type of fungus.

In most recipes with yeast, there are usually other ingredients such as sugar, salt, and flour. Both Ali and Brittany had used yeast in baking, and they wondered which ingredient made it grow fastest. They made three mixes in separate containers and added a package of dry yeast and ¼ cup warm water to each. Here are the results of their tests:

MIX WITH YEAST AND WATER	RESULTS AFTER AN HOUR
1. flour, sugar, salt	Lots of bubbles, smelled yeasty
2. flour, sugar	Two big bubbles
3. salt, sugar	A few small bubbles

After two hours, mix #1 had risen the most. There was one large bubble that had filled like a balloon. By the next day, it had burst. Brittany thought the yeast needed both flour and sugar to grow best. Do you agree? Repeat their test and see what you can discover.

Sparkling Counters and Squeaky Glasses

For thousands of years, people have been using soap. Soap works well as a cleanser, except that it is hard to rinse away completely. It leaves rings in a bathtub and a dull crud in freshly washed hair. Soap is made from oils and fats and strong bases. The bases used in soaps are also called alkali substances. One that is commonly used is lye, which comes from wood ash.

What do soaps and other cleansers really clean? As you follow your questions, make sure you experiment with items that no one will mind you messing with. For example, old rags are much better to use than your mother's finest tablecloth!

MOLECULAR ATTRACTION Like magnets, soap and detergent molecules have one end that repels and another that attracts. Instead of attracting or repelling magnets, the ends of soap molecules attract or repel water. The ends that repel water grab hold of oil and other fatty substances, which do not dissolve in water. The ends that attract water help the water loosen the dirt and hold the dirt suspended in the water until it is rinsed away. When loaded-up soap and detergent molecules are washed away with water, one end of the molecule holds on to the dirt and the other holds on to the water. Together the dirt, cleanser, and water all swirl down the drain, leaving clean dishes, clothes, or whatever else you've washed.

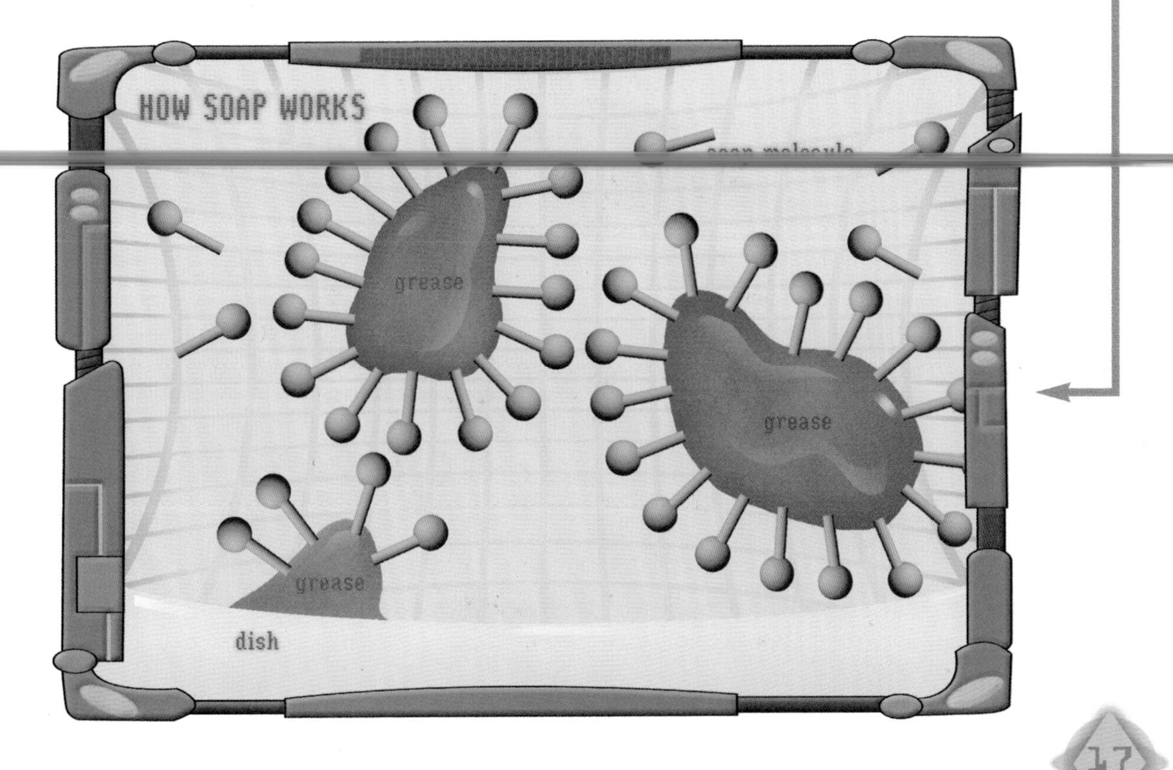

KID Experiments

MARKED CLOTH A well-stocked kitchen has a variety of cleansers. Nalani, Michelle, and Rachel were curious to know if any of these cleansers would remove spots made by a marker on cloth. (They knew that they should **never** mix ammonia with bleach. It makes a poison gas.)

After marking four pieces of cotton cloth with red and blue markers, they tried cleaning them with different substances. They conducted this test twice. Here are their results:

CLEANSER	RESULTS
1. ammonia	Made the markings paler, but did not remove them
2. dish detergent	Made the markings a little paler, but did not remove them
3. window cleaner	Did not change color of markings

The girls decided that none of these substances worked to remove marker stains. Maybe a spot remover would work better. What do you think? Why did each cleanser have the effect it did?

X AND Y Do you believe all those TV commercials that tell you that one brand of cleanser is better than all the others? Many detergents look and smell just the same. Do they wash the same?

Allison, Emily, and Katelyn conducted a test with two detergents that both smelled like lemons. One was marked X and the other Y. After they made a mess by smearing peanut butter on two different pans, the girls

washed each pan. To make sure the test was fair, they used the same temperature of water and the same scrubbing power. After one minute, they examined the pans to see how clean each one was. Detergent Y removed most of the gooey mess, but left a bit in one corner. Detergent X left a thin layer of grease over most of the pan. Katelyn thought Y probably worked better because it was more concentrated.

Allison, Emily, and Katelyn only conducted the test once. Do you think they would get the same results each time?

History of Detergent

In 1916 a German scientist named Fritz Gunther invented the world's first detergent. Unlike soaps, detergents are not made from fats. Other chemicals are used to attract and repel water instead.

No one was interested in detergents until World War I, when Germany ran short of the fats that they needed for making lubricants to keep machines running smoothly. Gunther's detergent was remembered and produced by chemists so that fat could be used to make lubricants instead of cleansers. Though the Germans stayed clean, they lost the war. The German cleanser, however, soon won the cleaning battle with soap. It didn't leave bathtub rings or any other residue. Before long, detergents were being used for everything from washing clothes to scrubbing dishes and mopping floors. Unfortunately, detergents were later discovered to be a cause of water pollution. Today's detergents are designed to work well without polluting waterways.

Gizmos and Gadgets

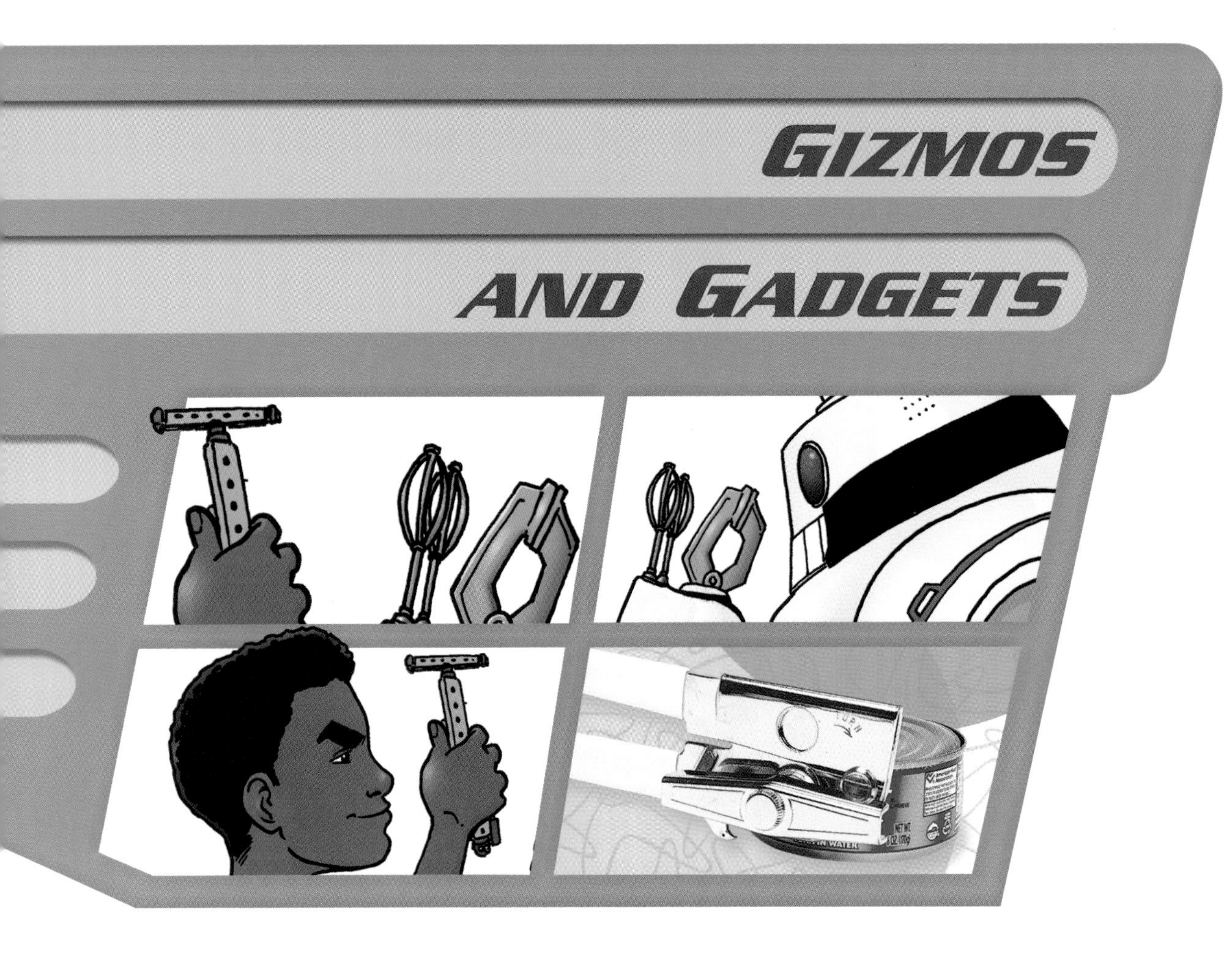

Sometimes kitchen drawers are so full of gadgets that you can barely open them. There are pizza slicers, garlic presses, bottle openers, and meat thermometers. Cupboards and counters are homes to blenders, food processors, waffle makers, and bread machines. These kitchen tools use everything from high-tech computer technology to basic old mechanical principles. A pizza cutter is simply a wheel with its edges sharpened like a blade. The wheel is then attached to an axle so that it can turn. A bottle opener is two levers with a gripper on one end. These everyday tools are ingenious inventions that are worth investigating. How does a corkscrew really work? Check it out.

Simple Machines

Wheels, gears, and levers are all simple machines that make work easier. A wheel is a rounded object that transfers motion with very little friction. Gears are wheels with teeth. They can change the speed and direction of movement. Levers magnify the amount of force used to pry open or lift an object. Many of the tools we use every day are a combination of wheels, gears, and levers. The pedals of a bike are attached to a bar, which is a lever. The lever turns a gear that moves a chain. The chain transfers the force of you pushing the pedals through gears to the back wheel, and the bike goes forward.

Kid Experiments

Homemade Beater Erector sets can be used to build all sorts of fun toys, but can you make a kitchen tool with one? After looking at all the parts in Alex's erector set, Alex and Nick decided they could invent an eggbeater. They attached a small electric motor to a battery pack and held the motor and battery pack in place inside a case made of metal panels. They attached a gear to the motor's shaft and bolted a crossbeam onto the gear. When the motor was turned on, the crossbeam whirled around and around like the blade on a beater.

Alex and Nick tested their beater in water, and it stirred the water up pretty well. To give it more beating action, they added another crossbeam, but two beams didn't seem to work as well as one. Then they attached a wire to the rotor to see if this would help with whipping power. It wasn't very effective, so they removed it.

The boys were pleased with their invention, but there were still some problems to work out. While it was beating, the motor swung from side to side. They thought that this might cause the beam to break or the glass they were beating water in to be chipped. Alex didn't want to try beating an egg, because the casing for the motor had lots of holes in it, like all erector set pieces do. He thought that the egg would fly up into the motor and clog it up. Do you have any ideas about how to eggproof the casing?

History of the Can Opener

Have you ever tried to open a can without some kind of can opener? It can be a difficult and even dangerous task. As crazy as it seems, canned foods were produced years before anyone invented a real can opener. First used by the British navy to store rations, tin canisters were ripped open by hungry sailors using everything from bayonets to bullets. Heavier than today's cans, they were no easy chore to open. One can even came with instructions to open it with a hammer and chisel!

The first patented can opener wasn't much better than a knife, and it was used only by the army. In 1870 American inventor William Lyman came up with the idea of a cutting wheel to slice along the rim of the can. This safe can opener became an immediate success and is the basic model that modern can openers are based on.

Examine a hand-operated can opener as you use it on a can. As you squeeze the handles together, notice how the sharp wheel cuts into the can. The handles are levers that enable you to force the wheel through the lid. As you turn the handle, notice how the gears grip the lid and rotate the can.

EXTREME TEMPERATURES

Like an arctic explorer, you can investigate the formation of crystals or the effect of extreme cold on tropical fruits. You can observe the effects of heat on foods or other substances, as long as you are sure you are not going to stink up the house or, worse yet, cause a fire. Be safe whenever using the stove and work under the supervision of a parent or local firefighter.

HEATING AND COOLING The movement of atoms, the tiny particles that make up all things, causes heat. When heat is applied to a substance, the atoms in it move faster. Cold is the absence of heat.

Heat can change substances. Heat added to water can make it boil and turn into steam, which is water in a gaseous state. When enough heat is taken away from water, its atoms slow down and the liquid water becomes solid ice.

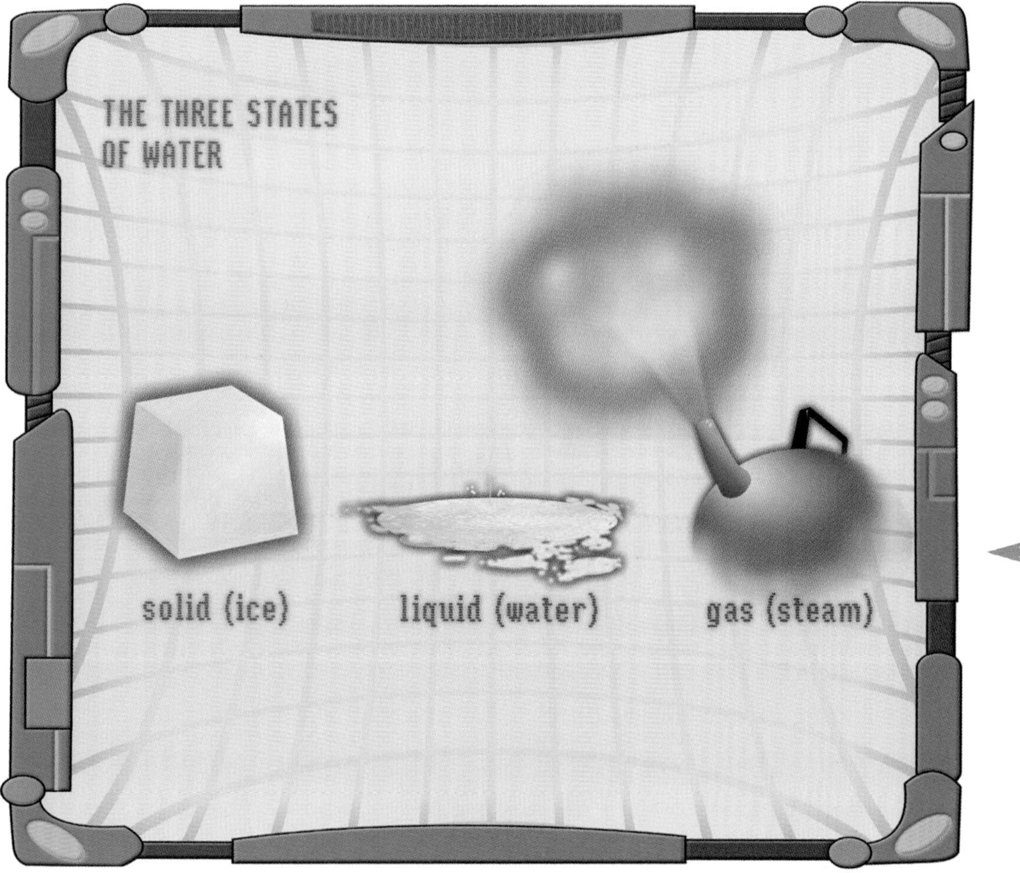

KID Experiments

BUBBLED POPSICLES Have you ever played with a frothy broth of soapy bubbles? While Claire and Michelle were having fun making bubbles with dish detergent and water, they noticed that the bubbles lasted for quite a while. The girls wondered if the bubbles would go away if they put the froth in the freezer. To make the bubbles easier to see, they added blue food coloring to the next batch of bubbles they made. Then they stored the blue bubbles in the freezer for a couple of days. What do you think happened?

After carefully examining the block of ice, Claire and Michelle noticed that there were many little bubbles near the top. Claire thought it looked like an ice pond that isn't safe to skate on. The top layer of ice was thin and contained bubbles. The bottom was solid ice. The ice at the bottom was blue. The bubbles didn't go away, but they had shrunk. Claire thought that the cold somehow made the bubbles get smaller. Why do you think the bubbles shrank? How big a bubble do you think you could freeze?

ZAPPED SNACKS Most kids heat up soup, pizza, or other foods in microwave ovens without a second thought. But Nathan and Emily had some questions about what this heating machine could do. They wondered if they could explode a grape by heating it up.

To prevent the microwave from being coated with grape goo, they placed the grape inside a paper towel before zapping it. After thirty seconds of heating, they checked the grape and discovered that it had shrunk. It was hot and had a small burn mark. They put it back in and cooked it for another five minutes. The grape began to smell. When they took it out, all that was left was the black, burned shell of a grape, like a severely toasted marshmallow. Nathan and Emily agreed that you couldn't blow up a grape in a microwave, but you sure could burn one and stink up the room.

FROZEN GLOP When he made gloppy mixtures, Kyle noticed that they often separated into layers. Would this happen if he froze them? In a bowl, he mixed sugar, salt, vegetable oil, vinegar, food coloring, and baking soda. He set this gloppy soup in the freezer and checked it the next morning. It had indeed separated into definite layers! By examining the frozen glop closely, he could tell what some of the layers were. The top layer contained the food coloring, the next layer was the vegetable oil, and below that was the vinegar. At the very bottom was a thick sludge that Kyle guessed was made up of salt, sugar, and possibly baking soda. He repeated the test three more times. Each time he got the same results. Kyle thought that the mixture separated into layers because the ingredients couldn't stay together due to chemical reactions. What do you think?

Temperamental Cookies How will cookies bake at different temperatures? wondered Ali, Nicole, Brittany, and Nalani. The girls baked their chocolate chip cookie dough at 300°F, 350°F, and 400°F. Each batch was placed on the middle rack of the oven and baked for seven minutes. The first batch, baked at 300°F, came out a little too crisp, and the girls didn't think they tasted very good. The second batch, baked at 350°F, was just right. When they raised the temperature to 400°F, the third batch burned.

Brittany had thought that the first batch would be gooey instead of crispy. None of the girls could explain why this happened. Do you have any ideas? Maybe you could repeat the experiment and see if you get the same results. At least it would be a good excuse for making some cookies!

History of the Microwave

Like many inventions, the microwave oven was the result of an accident. In 1946 Dr. Percy Spencer, an engineer at Raytheon Company, was testing a magnetron tube when he melted a candy bar in his pocket. Magnetron tubes were used in radar equipment. Though Spencer knew they could give off heat, he had felt no heat. He was intrigued. How did the candy bar melt? Instead of going home and changing into clean pants, he got some popcorn kernels and set them close to the tube. After a couple of minutes, the kernels were popping all over the floor. Next he tried cooking an egg. It exploded, shooting its insides onto the face of a fellow worker who was watching the experiment. Fortunately, he wasn't hurt.

The explosion made Spencer realize that the egg was cooked from the inside out. The electromagnetic waves from the magnetron tube made water molecules move faster, causing them to heat up. As the molecules heated up inside the eggshell, they moved so much that the shell burst. Raytheon Company produced the first commercial microwave oven. It was the size of a refrigerator, with a small oven compartment. Modern microwave ovens can also cook eggs, but think twice about the mess you'll make before you explode eggs in your family's microwave oven!

RUBBER PIZZA

Years ago, all pizza was baked fresh in big brick pizzeria ovens. You couldn't even buy a frozen pizza at the market. Now there are dozens of brands of supermarket pizzas, but what's the best way to heat them up for a meal? They can be reheated in a flash in a microwave, but the crust often ends up as rubbery as a tennis ball. Using a traditional gas or electric oven takes longer, but gives the pizza a crusty crust.

Three food scientists at the University of Massachusetts wondered what changes take place during the two different cooking methods to lead to such different textures of crust. As they test-heated one pizza after another, they took measurements and found out that the pizzas dried out more along the edges than in the center, no matter which way they were heated. In the microwave oven, the pizzas not only heated up faster, but they also dried out sooner and shrank more. Using special instruments, the scientists were able to detect changes

in the structure of the pizza dough in microwaved pizzas, such as the entanglement of dough particles. Was this why the pizza became rubbery? That's what the pizza research team proposed. They thought that slower heating and less drying out allowed the crust to swell and loosen, making a lighter crust. The fast heating and drying out in a microwave probably caused the dough to shrink and become tight and leathery. They discovered that heating pizza for less than two minutes in a microwave made it a lot less rubbery.

Though the scientists learned about some of the changes that occur in microwaved pizza dough, they still didn't have any clue how to make a dough that would be less tough. What changes could they make in dough recipes to create a crust that doesn't rubberize in the microwave? You may one day discover the answer. Until then, heating frozen pizza is still a choice between quickly warmed but rubbery dough, and a slowly heated, crispy crust.

CHICKEN, ONIONS, AND ROSES

Look around your kitchen. If you look carefully, you'll see that it's like a museum of plant and animal parts. Instead of looking at those parts in display cases, you'll discover them in jars, cans, boxes, and bags.

Plants have four basic parts: roots, stems, leaves, and fruits. Animals have muscles that we eat. Which of these body parts can you find in your kitchen?

KITCHEN Anatomy

Surgeons need to study human anatomy for years and years before they are ready to operate on patients. To be a chicken surgeon and discover how a chicken's body works, you don't have to have major training, but you **must** follow some basic safety precautions.

- Wash your hands carefully before and after this exercise. Do not put your fingers in your mouth while you are examining the chicken. Raw meat can harbor bacteria that make people sick.
- **Use a knife only when supervised by an adult!** When you carve the chicken, be very careful how you use the knife. Always be aware of where your fingers are. You want to carve the chicken, not yourself.

YOU WILL NEED:

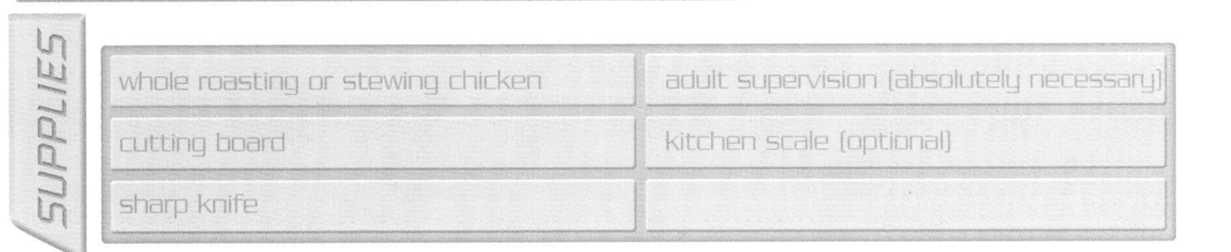

SUPPLIES

whole roasting or stewing chicken	adult supervision (absolutely necessary)
cutting board	kitchen scale (optional)
sharp knife	

If you have eaten chickens or turkeys, you already have some experience with the anatomy of a bird. As you examine your chicken, think about the chicken parts you have eaten. If you have a kitchen scale, weigh your chicken before operating.

Skin Tour

bump search: A plucked chicken looks like it has goose bumps, but of course they must be chicken bumps! These bumps are the follicles where the feathers grew. Most birds have feathers only on certain sections of their skin. Can you find areas that have bumps, and others that are mostly smooth? Bumps are bigger where bigger feathers were attached. How do the bumps on the wings and tail compare with the bumps on other parts?

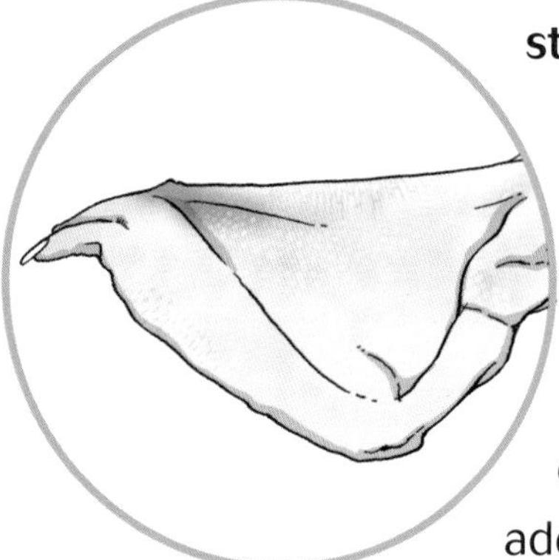

stretchy covering: If you pull at your skin, you'll notice how it stretches. How stretchy is bird skin? Pull at the skin on different parts of the chicken. Check out the skin on the wings. These thin flaps are like the thin metal on an airplane's wing. The skin provides the chicken with a flat surface for liftoff without adding very much weight.

fat fowls: How much fat does your chicken have? Very carefully peel off the skin and you'll discover deposits of yellow fat. Cut off all the fat and weigh it. How does it compare to the total weight of the chicken? Where did you find the most fat? Where do you think you have most of your fat?

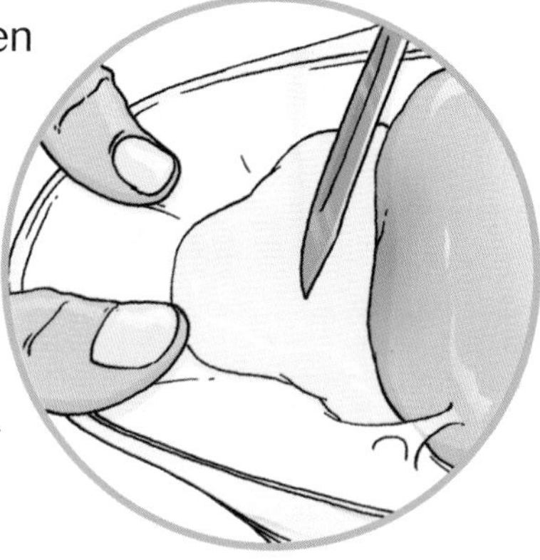

Joint Actions

Have you ever thought about how your joints allow you to move around? When you flex your fingers, rotate your arms, and curl your toes, your body bends at joints between your bones. Birds have joints too. Some of their joints are more flexible than people's are. For example, some birds can twist their heads around more than people can. Some of their other joints are stiffer than people's are.

back bends: When you bend over, your back bends. When you try to bend the back of a chicken, you'll discover that it is as stiff as a board. A stiff back helps the bird stay straight while flying.

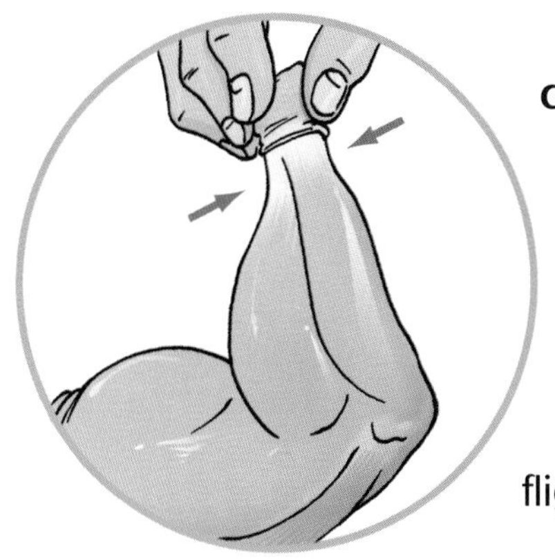

chicken run: Move a chicken leg back and forth. Compare its movement with that of your own legs. When you play tag, you can dart from side to side or dash forward or backwards. Bird legs work best for forward movement, such as when a bird is running or leaping into flight.

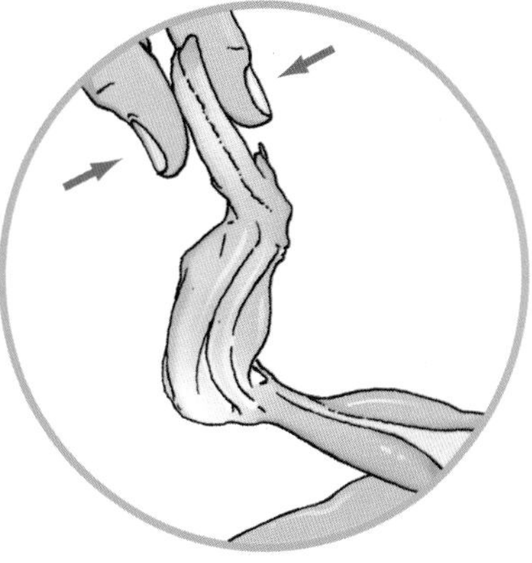

in flight: Notice how the joints on a chicken's wing allow it to fold up into a neat little Z when it is not in use. Stretch the wing out and rotate it to see how it might move in flight.

Muscular Machines

Birds, like other animals, are machines with muscles. Muscles move everything from wings to bills to toes.

weight lifters: People who press weights soon develop bigger biceps (arm muscles) and pectoral muscles (chest muscles), but their muscles are small compared to the flight muscles of a bird. Check out the size of the breast muscles (breast meat) on your chicken. These muscles may make up to one-fifth of the total weight of a bird! Chickens have been bred for extra-big breast muscles. The muscles actually weigh the bird down and keep it from flying well!

red or white: Birds have two basic types of muscle tissue, white (light) and red (dark). White muscle is good for strong, but short, bursts of energy. Heavy birds like chickens and quail have white flight muscles, while hawks and other constant flyers have dark flight muscles. Look at the drumsticks (legs) of a chicken. Are there large red muscles? As anyone knows who has tried to catch a chicken, they can run for a long time! Where else can you find red or white meat?

drumstick strings: As you cut into the muscles on a drumstick, you will discover stringlike structures called tendons. These enable the chicken to use the large muscles on the upper leg to move the lower part of the leg. What muscles can you feel when you wiggle your toes?

GUTSY INVESTIGATIONS

A butchered chicken has most of its guts missing, but you can usually find the heart, gizzard, and liver inside the main cavity of the bird.

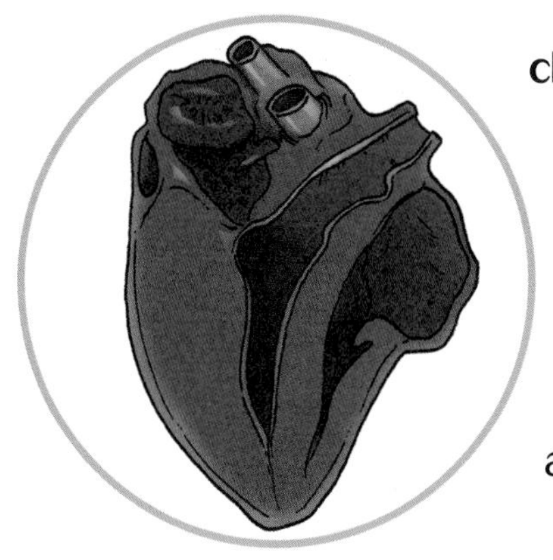

chicken hearted: Like most hearts, a chicken's is not shaped like a valentine. It is shaped more like a toy top. If you slice it in half, you can see the main cavity that blood is pumped through. As you carve the chicken, look for tubes. These are veins and arteries that pipe blood through the body.

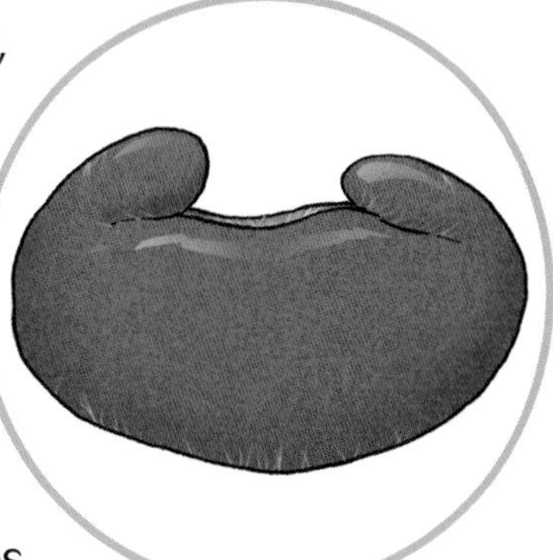

nut grinder: Unlike us, birds lack teeth. They can peck or tear at food with their bills, but the food is ground up in the gizzard. This saddle-bag-shaped organ is made of very strong muscles that can actually crack nuts. Chickens often swallow gravel, which settles in the gizzard and enables them to pulverize really tough food. Cut the gizzard open to see if you can discover any small pebbles.

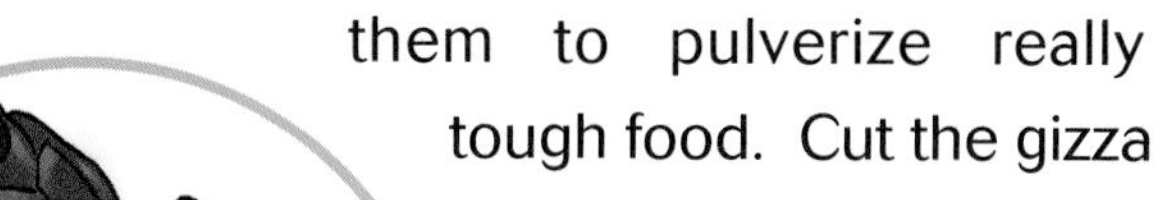

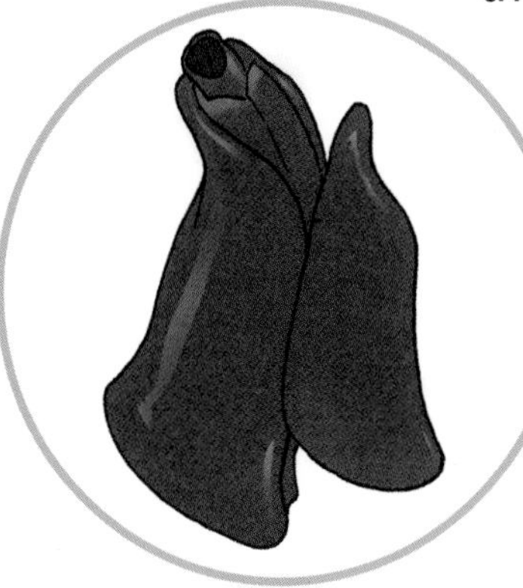

storage and filter: Livers act as filters to extract waste and poisons from the blood. They also store excess sugars.

Skeleton Soup

As you carve meat off your chicken, you will discover bones beneath the muscles. If you cook the bones in water, you can get a much clearer look at them. Boil the bones in a large pot of water for a couple of hours, or until the meat falls off. Cool the broth and remove the bones. You can use the broth and meat to make chicken soup and use the bones for study. On the next page is a diagram of a chicken skeleton. See which bones you can find.

muscle bone: The sternum, or breastbone, is the large bone where the wing muscles are attached. All flying birds have a large ridge running down the center of the sternum. The ridge is what the wing muscles are attached to.

joint puzzle: The leg and wing bones are long and have bulblike ends. See if you can fit any of the bones together at these joints.

wishbone wishes: A V-shaped bone called the furcula, or wishbone, joins the shoulder bones of a bird. See if you can find it.

backbone counts: The backbone is composed of small bones called vertebrae that are joined together. How many can you find? Unlike our vertebrae, some of the chicken vertebrae are fused together. Fused vertebrae make chickens' backs less flexible than people's.

light gear: Bird bones are much lighter than our bones because they are hollow. Use some kitchen shears to cut a bone in half so you can examine the inside.

Other creatures to examine and eat: crabs, squid, whole fish.

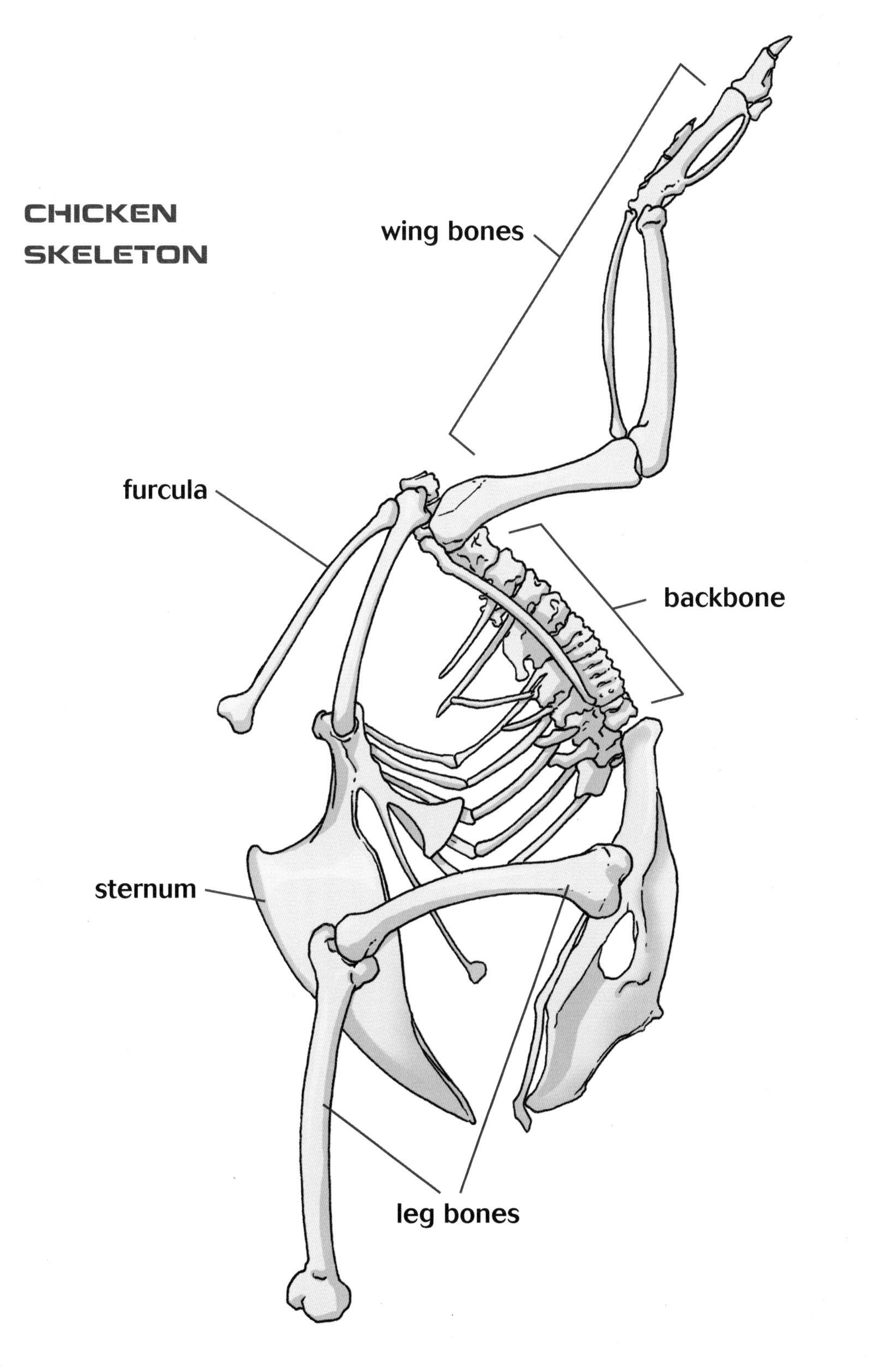
CHICKEN
SKELETON
wing bones
furcula
backbone
sternum
leg bones

KITCHEN Classification

PLANT FAMILY REUNIONS Kitchen cupboards and refrigerators are homes to parts of plants from a wide variety of plant families. Scientists sort species of plants into groups of similar plants called families. When you gather together parts of plants that are in the same family, you might be able to detect some of the qualities they have in common.

Plants in the carrot family, for instance, have a strong aroma. They also have fernlike leaves and hard, dry seeds with ridges. Search through the kitchen for some of these plants or plant parts. Do they have the characteristics you expect to find in the carrot family?

CARROT FAMILY

anise seeds	celery seeds	parsley
caraway seeds	cilantro	parsnips
carrots	coriander	
celery	cumin seeds	

Some other families of plants that we eat are the cabbage, pea, and rose families. Below are common members of each family. See if you can discover some of the characteristics of each family. (Look for answers on page 48.)

PEA FAMILY

- alfalfa sprouts
- black-eyed peas
- green beans
- lentils
- peanuts
- pinto beans
- sweet peas
- lima beans

ROSE FAMILY

- almonds
- apples
- apricots
- blackberries
- cherries
- nectarines
- peaches
- pears
- plums
- raspberries
- strawberries

CABBAGE FAMILY

- bok choy
- broccoli
- brussels sprouts
- cabbage
- cauliflower
- mustard greens
- mustard seeds
- radishes

PLANT PARTS

Plants have four basic parts: roots, stems, leaves, and fruits. Some of these parts can be hard to identify. Examine these tricky plant parts in your own kitchen:

ONIONS: Bulbs have roots, a tiny stem, and leaf bases. Leave an onion out of the refrigerator for long enough, and leaves will grow.

POTATOES: Potatoes may look like roots, but they're really very fleshy underground stems called tubers. If a tuber is left out on the counter for a while, it will sprout.

BROCCOLI: Buds that will open up to become flowers make up the head of a broccoli plant. Fruits develop from flowers. A head of broccoli left in the refrigerator for long enough might actually bloom. The green buds will open, revealing small, yellow-petaled flowers.

PUMPKINS, PEA PODS, CUCUMBERS, AND TOMATOES: Fruits have seeds inside them. Even though we call these "vegetables," they are all fruits.

WALNUTS, ALMONDS, AND PECANS: Fruits of some trees are dry and protected by a hard shell. We call them nuts.

Glossary

acid: a sour-tasting substance that can be dissolved in water. Acids react with bases to form salts.

alkali: any of several basic salts found in soil or water

anatomy: the structure of a plant or animal

base: a substance that usually feels soapy and reacts with acids to form salts

electromagnetic waves: waves of energy created by electric or magnetic fields

family: a group of living things with similar characteristics

follicle: a small pit on the skin from which a hair or a feather grows

furcula: the "wishbone" of a bird that joins the shoulder bones

litmus paper: a type of paper that turns a different color when in contact with an acid or a base

molecule: one or more atoms making up the smallest part of a compound that has all the characteristics of that substance

pH: a measurement of the acidity or basicity of a substance

Metric Conversion Table

When you know:	Multiply by:	To find:
inches (in.)	2.54	centimeters (cm)
feet (ft.)	0.305	meters (m)
teaspoons (tsp.)	4.929	milliliters (ml)
tablespoons (tbsp.)	14.79	milliliters (ml)
cups (c.)	236.6	milliliters (ml)
quarts (qt.)	0.946	liters (l)
ounces (oz.)	28.35	grams (g)

To convert degrees Fahrenheit (°F) to degrees Celsius (°C), subtract 32, then multiply by $\frac{5}{9}$.

Index

acids, 10, 11
anatomy, 37–43

bases, 10, 11, 16
bones, 39, 42–43

chicken, 36, 37–43
cleansers. *See* detergent
comparisons, 8, 13–15, 18–20, 31–32, 44–45
cooking, 14, 31–32, 42
cooling, 6, 26, 27, 28, 30

detergent, 10, 16, 17–20, 21, 28
dirt, 10, 16, 17

fruits, 36, 44–45, 46

gears, 23, 24, 25

heating, 26, 27, 29, 31–32, 34–35, 42

ice, 6, 27, 28, 30

leaves, 36, 44–45, 46
levers, 22, 23, 25

microwave ovens, 29, 33, 34–35
muscles, 36, 39–40

note taking, 8, 9

observation, 38–43, 44–45. *See also* tests

plants, 36, 44–45, 46

questions, 7–8, 13, 14, 19, 24, 28, 30, 31, 38–40, 42

roots, 36, 44, 46
rules, 5–6, 18, 37

scientific method, 9
scientists, 21, 25, 33, 34–35
skin, 38
soap. *See* detergent
stems, 36, 45, 46

tests, 8, 12–15, 18–20, 24, 28–32, 34–35, 38–42

wheels, 22, 23

ANSWERS FROM PAGE 45:
cabbage family: parts have a spicy taste, leaves have toothed edges, seeds are tiny
pea family: seeds are rounded, seeds are found in pods, seeds split in two when soaked
rose family: sweet fleshy fruits, seeds pointed at each end

Photo Acknowledgments
All photographs appear courtesy of Todd Strand/Independent Picture Service except the photograph on p. 33 (bottom), which has been reproduced with the permission of © Bettmann/CORBIS.